PRAISE FOR *THEN GONE*

"Ed Hack's sonnets navigate a contemplated lifetime's worth of *sic transits* and *ubi sunts* to reach—in their clever, revealing turns—moments of clarity about 'The things we carry along with us.' *Then Gone* begins with the realities of retirement and relocation, but transports us far beyond quiet strolls in the subtropical sunset. This book of 100 sonnets divided into 11 sections is a book of poems interested in *destinations,* in the intersection of self and light and love, in a heart that after awful failures was awakened to its deepest needs by a human voice. These exquisitely well-crafted sonnets speak, in language that smooths and embellishes their solid structure and rhyme, of and for 'we exiles inexplicable / to any who are young,' those elders for whom 'Time's a dream / of passing days.' These powerful and moving poems glow with ghosts and shine with wisdom-inflected wonder at the totality of human existence in all its fleeting beauty and dubious purpose. His world is 'an endless masquerade of balances' filled with the whispers of the bedroom and the anguished cries of strangers half a globe away. His people and his poems breathe, gasp, die, grieve, sing and challenge us to go on.

—George Guida, author of *Zen of Pop* and *New York and Other Lovers*

THEN GONE

THEN GONE

100 Sonnets

Ed Hack

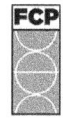

Full Court Press
Englewood Cliffs, New Jersey

First Edition

Copyright © 2022 by Ed Hack

All rights reserved. No part of this book may be reproduced or transmitted in any form or by any means electronic or mechanical, including by photocopying, by recording, or by any information storage and retrieval system, without the express permission of the author, except where permitted by law.

Published in the United States of America by Full Court Press, 601 Palisade Avenue, Englewood Cliffs, NJ 07632
fullcourtpress.com

ISBN 978-1-953728-05-0
Library of Congress Control No. 2022911531

Book design by Barry Sheinkopf

All interior art courtesy of Barry Sheinkopf

For Franny
as always

And for all my children

Preface

Why sonnets?

For years, until eight years ago, I wrote free verse, poems free of established forms, meters, of traditional stanza-types. The poet makes it up as he or she goes on, finding for each poem a specific music created by word choice and placement. That music is both the structure and meaning of each poem.

I had taught Shakespeare for many years, the plays, the two long narrative poems, and the sonnets. Each student had to memorize a sonnet and then say it to the class—*say* it, not recite it, since each sonnet is a voice saying something to someone with all the nuance and variations of emphasis that one uses when saying something important to someone else. So my work was to lean closer to the sonnets than I ever had to catch each one's voice, to hear not only what it was saying but how it was breathing through the lines from start to finish— the stops and starts, the hesitations, turns of mind, allusions simmering, and a back-story teasingly surfacing. At least to me.

So when I was tired of free verse, sometime after I retired, the challenge of writing Shakespearean sonnets rose in my mind. And, I guess, bubbling around in my mind was *Those who can't, teach. . . .* So I studied the sonnets differently, as a poet, starting with confidently writing iambic pentameter, with the help of a knowledgeable friend. That took a little more than six months. And then the rest of it, which I am still exploring, some 2,000 sonnets later.

Fourteen lines of iambic pentameter: three quatrains and a couplet.

No more. No less.

A random sampling of ten of my sonnets shows that the number of words per poem varies from 107 to 126, with the most ranging from 112 to 120 words. 120 or fewer words to create a convincing emotional or intellectual moment that is complex, clever, nuanced, and powerful. Memorable. The sonnet, certainly as Shakespeare used and developed it, is a layered close-up of a human experience. That is the challenge that I wanted, the tradition I wanted to be a part of, the wall I wanted to lean against.

Originally an Italian form, the sonnet was brought to England by Sir Thomas Wyatt in the 1530s, where it became a popular lyric form for love poems. In 1609 Shakespeare's *Sonnets* was published, and its 154 sonnets set the standard and the structure for all the poets who have chosen his form. His puns, rhymes, ironies, ambiguities, turns of phrase and allusions, and dramatic use of meter to enhance the meaning and the music of each poem, continue to set the standard for poets. They set it for me.

Shakespeare's sonnets are the template I chose. To use the form is to be part of the sonnet's long history—it is to be inspired and challenged by that history, to be a part of it, to try to master the sonnet's possible music, the limitless worlds beyond the love poem (but also including it) that can be constructed within a tightly limited form that has all kinds of internal elasticities, and grow as a poet and person, to imagine, think, and feel more deeply. To be less alone as I face the blank page. Each day I give myself another chance to write a better, truer, deeper, more probing, moving sonnet, to write a portrait which is also an X-ray, which is also an exploration, which is also a meditation that, hopefully, catches fire in the reader's mind and, because of that fire, the reader sees and feels and lives for a little while—maybe longer than a little—within that sonnet's world.

—E.H.

Table of Contents

Leaving / Arriving

Two Days To Go, 1
Old Friends, 2
The Heart Will Not Forget, 3
Cleaning Up Contacts, 4
The Ways I Knew, 5
The Light Down Here, 6
Mentors, 7
Refugees, 8
What's Possible, 9
Joy, 10
From Night, 11
Dead, 12
Far Away, 13
Times Ten, 14
Amah, 15
The Beach At Night, 16
Begins Again, 17
At The Diner, 18

Early / Morning

3 a.m., 21
Up Too Early, 22

What Waits, 23
Like This, 24
Coffee, 25
Mother, 26
Always Waiting, 27
Call, 28
Difficult, 29
The Spark, 30
Exempt From Death, 31
Up From Sleep, 32
A Step Away, 33
Signs And Wonders, 34
Not A Single Instant, 35

Spring / Summer

What's Coming, 39
Arrivals, 40
What Time Will Bring, 41
Cherry Tree, 42
More Than Sixty Years Ago, 43
July 1, 44

Autumn

Near, 47
All The Proof, 48
Winter Geese, 49

The End Of Day, 50
Autumn Rain, 51

Day's End

Autumn By The River, 55
Can't Sleep, 56
The Gloaming, 57
But Not, 58

Death / Afterwards

Before The End, 61
First Night, 62
Billy, 63
Friends Walking, 64
Air, 65
More, 66

Winter

First Time In Days, 69
The Coldest Morning, 70
Magic You Can Trust, 71
The Heart Learns, 72
Weather For Hawks, 73
What He Found, 74
A Kind Of Dust, 75

Nature

On Hold, 79
The Seers, 80
The Cost, 81
Alchemy, 82
A Deer, 83
Weathers, 84
Full Flight, 85
Cannot Be Appeased, 86

Old Bones

Ghosts, 89
Circles, 90
Not A Blur, 91
Before I Blow The Candles Out, 92

Domestic Life

The Fan, 95
Hush, 96
A Shape Of Ice, 97
At The Dentist, 98
Montecito, California: A Photo From Above, 99
Under Anesthesia, 101
My Sin, 102
Part Of Me, 103
The 24th, 104

Hard Day, 105
What We Learned, 106
Our Tribe, 107
Failure, 108
Venice, 109
Behind The Curtain, 110
Again, 111
Steps, 112
Addict, 113
Before The Brink, 114
No More El Dorados?, 115
Untitled, 116

Love

Happy Birthday, 119
The Study, 120
This Human Life, 121
Our Sunday, 122
Flight 235 From Atlantic City, 123
Knitting, 124

Leaving / Arriving

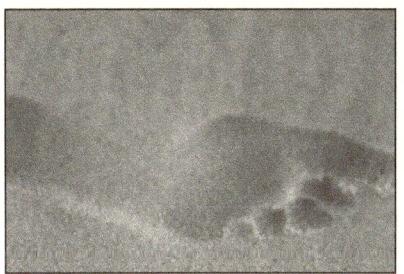

Two Days To Go

Two days before the moving truck arrives.
I reach. I touch the chair. My feet are on
the floor. I smell the coffee brew. My wife's
asleep. This is, and this is not, my home.
In hours I'll have to ask if I can sit
right here. The garden's soaked a lush, deep green.
The irises' unearthly tongues now sip
the chilly air. In hours this will have been
my home: the flowers, bricks, and every nail,
the stairs that creak, the door that sticks, the tile
that cools my feet, my name upon the mail—
this everything to me will soon expire
like smoke into the light, and other souls
will find their lives where I was healed, made whole.

Old Friends

The things we take along with us. The way
we cannot not have them—the Buddha head,
the elephant, the wooden fish—displayed
as talismans—things in their place: instead
of accident, design, intention's hope,
the quiet of control. I know the fool
I am, that luck is only so much smoke,
but who knows what might be the crucial tool
that moves the gods to not be cruel or sneak
our lives away? The face with wings that guards
the door—another creature that I keep—
perhaps holds off what's hanging in the stars.
My tiny zoo is deaf and dumb and kind,
old friends who help me fend off the malign.

The Heart Will Not Forget
(for A)

We run because we want to live. Because
we feel but cannot name the scar that burns
our blood to steam. Young eyes don't miss the flaws
that mar their elders' lives, and flight affirms
the truths the heart cannot explain. Yet home
is home, the newel post in the hall, the motes
in nineteenth-century air, the cedar bones
that braced her like a sailing ship afloat
through Time atop the rise above the bay.
That, too, the heart will not forget, the peace
beyond, below the noise. And there it stays,
at home, in harbor while the winds increase
as all speeds by. With luck, with work, we slow
to silences that house taught us to know.

Cleaning Up Contacts

Deleting names. A past that's moribund.
Defunct. Defective. Any other *D*s?
Dejected? No, though this is not great fun.
Erasure—one beyond the *D*s—agrees
with what is real, and that's what really counts.
I should have walked away, just been polite.
I should. I should. . . I. . .what a sad account,
pathetic soul who couldn't get things right.
I see a name. No face pops up, no voice.
Where was I then? How stoned was I? What role
that day? A fool is one who has no choice.
You waste life's time, you've got to pay the toll.
Default. I'm smiling at the irony.
Now back to work, now that I'm up to *E*.

The Ways I Knew

Who knew that later on I'd have to learn
another world? The habits of one place,
what I expect—the corners where I turned,
that light in trees, those windows in that space
between the roof and walk, the grass that yard
has never grown, the brick that's weathered storms,
the narrow street that runs with rain, the guard
when kids are leaving school, and when they're gone,
the quiet of the intersection. Shouts
from Jessica, who's playing with a friend;
Ariana, with Bear on the leash, out
of school with phone glued to her ear. The bend
my street must take before the traffic light:
the ways I knew where I belonged at night.

The Light Down Here

A new week starts in our new home. The light's
the same, but not at all. A thousand miles
from what we knew, I see this light sets sights
on what it shines upon—the palms, the piles
of bleached, white block, the blonde communities
behind their walls, the sleekly manicured
environs of the rich, cool luxuries,
svelte expectations of the self-assured.
On other roads, reality: baked hot
and flaking walls, used furniture and cars,
the scraping-by, the working-hard for not
enough, uneasy hopes, and endless scars.
What you see is what you—you know the rest:
But here? Down here, the light is merciless.

Mentors

It's my turn now to be invisible.
This honor's for the old, the horde of us
down here, we exiles inexplicable
to any who are young—what we were once.
It seems so long ago, so very near—
a blink, and I'm in Latin 101,
or blind with urgency, insane with fear,
I close the door, put on my pack, and run.
A billion histories of love, disease,
and luck, of work and war, of needs and dreams,
accomplishments and legacies—all these
and more achieved by white-haired figurines,
bent backs, frail knees—my mentors on this path
to stone that says my name and date I passed.

Refugees

Behind the 80 doors are 80 fates,
inheritors, responsible for more.
That strange, apparently ironic man
who laughs alone at what he understands,
and he at 93, exhausted by
his chemistry, who can't get out of bed.
And she with jaunty hat and walker wheels
who dresses up each day, and he, whose deal
with life I will not guess, and they who've cared
so many years about each other's souls,
and she who sits alone for hours but seems
as sane as light. This is where Time's a dream
of passing days, and we're all refugees
en route—some lame, some not, some on their knees.

What's Possible

At 93, I don't think that he knows
much more than all he knew when he was young.
How is that possible? The years go slow,
go fast with wrongs that cannot be undone—
not now—for they are so long gone. What's Time
to him? His waking up? The cane that he
must use? The bike he cannot ride? His mind,
preoccupied by all he could not be?
One child dead. The other in a home.
Divorced. A history of almost-there,
of never knowing quite enough. Alone
with thoughts he cannot trust that scare
him to his bones, that shake his soul,
that tell him that he's useless and too old.

Joy

She's limping by. She limps by everyday
to practice being almost who she used
to be before the stroke. She walks and sways
in broken stutter step. She had to choose—
she made her choice. So she does not give up—
not morning, midday, evening, every day,
year round. Her words are blurred; she doesn't stop
until she's said what's on her mind. I say,
"How are you, Joy?" She smiles the way she smiles.
We talk, then she continues on her task,
across the catwalk, down the stairs. The miles
add up, each willful step. She won't relax—
she does her work. I've not heard her complain,
not once. I cannot even guess her pain.

From Night

The sun is out is not a metaphor,
although it is. And shadows on the lawn
explain what physics is and are a door
to how the self's contrived, that we are born
into the light, which means that we were torn
from night. It's always two for one. And more.
So many use their hurt to hurt, so worn
by life they keep their scorpions in store,
defending their illusions at the cost
of someone else. I know a man like that
who tastes each day the acid of his loss,
a cynic always ready to attack,
who'd ruin another man if he felt cause,
convince himself it's all the other's flaws.

Dead

A man I just began to know has killed
himself. It was a green and sun-filled day.
He shot himself right through his head, outside,
so he'd be found. He didn't want to hide,
wind up a putrid mess. This is F's guess.
One sentence in his blog announced the news—
a friend had written it. Why did he choose
his death, *this* death? Why did he have to lose
his only chance to see the sky, the light
that breaks the grip of night? What awful blight
had seized his soul? What had he done that he
could not forget or face or live to see
another second of his life? Predawn.
A lone birds calls. Again. Before day's born.

Far Away
(for AP)

A butterfly? A bird? Too far away
for me to know, but orange wings begin
the day amid lush green amid the gray
of rain-soaked days. All's still right now. No wind
disturbs the heavy trees. No deer surprise
the eye. The grass is calm as sleep. A dear
friend sends me news about the old whose lives
are pared away to truth. That's coming near
and will arrive. I'll see. We all will see.
And all the insane arguments, the *rights*
we so defend, will fail, and so must we,
defeated by the deeper facts, the light
that we ignore. The stupid and the smart
are one, at last, when they play their last part.

Times Ten

The same old nonsense, honed by all the years
perfecting it. That too is here, times ten.
A foolishness and meanness, too, the fears
they've turned to arguments to bend,
to skew the complex world to meet their needs.
For all their years, so little learned except
their pain. Perhaps that is a kind of greed,
for this is all they have, so to forget,
forgive, to ask if there is something new,
another way to see, is to betray
what they have left, the one thing that is true
that's only theirs, that no one takes away.
So easy in this world to lose yourself,
to think you are your hurt and nothing else.

Amah

Amah, she asks. *What are those in the sky*
that look like Mama's bright, white shiny stones?
This is the night. That means that day went by.
And what is Time? When things that were are done?
And that's the river over there. The tracks
that hold the train that rushes in like rain—
I mean where there's a storm. The night is black.
The day is hot. They're not at all the same.
Amah, am I a ghost? I heard the maid Le Mei
say that. What does that mean? I'm not a ghost.
I'm me. You're holding me. When will the day
come back? For breakfast can I have some toast?
In China long ago as stories are,
she slept in Amah's arms beneath the stars.

―――――――――――――

(Amah: a nursemaid in China, East Asia, and India)

The Beach At Night

The wash and rush from distances beyond
all common sense, the constancy of it,
forever down there on the beach. The calm,
like falling into sleep. The plane's lights flick
like fireflies against an ink-black night.
The buoys blink, go dark, then blink again.
There's nothing here but everything—the slight,
the grand, are both mysterious. Both *then*
and *now* are cancelled by the rise and fall
and crash, the rise and fall and crash, the sound
of Time, its heart, the pulse beneath it all,
the ocean's rush, the way the dark resounds
and echoes in our bones, the mind attuned
until it only hears the crash and *boom*.

Begins Again

An accidental music charms the day
as stained glass sun backlights the yellow leaves'
translucent gold. Meandering, the way
the chimes perfume the air, release then cease,
then play again, like clouds across the eye
or writing on the water by the wind.
In Florida, that tree still shapes the sky.
So here I am again, and so it all begins
again—this cast of characters, the end-
game of so many lives, uncounted tales
like leaves blown off the Tree Of Life to blend
into the mulch of spring. The sun's the grail
that brought us here, and Time's the winnowing
of Truth and memory these years might bring.

At The Diner

The clash of silverware, the clink of spoon
against the sturdy China mug, the rag
that's cleaning up the rail, the TV doom-
scenarios of Sunday news from flacks,
agendas in their eyes. The breakfast crowd
is chowing down, the single men, the gal
who knows the waitresses, who talks about
her ex who couldn't cook, the sweet chorale
of diner noise, the families with kids,
the cash drawer's bell, the orders handed in,
the plates with scrambled eggs and bacon strips,
home fries and buttered toast. The day begins
with faith in food, the habits of our lives.
So far, so good. If only we were wise.

Early / Morning

3 a.m.

The dead, the used-to-be, the faded days
surround me in the dark of 3 a.m.
The iron law that all must go the way
to others' memory I understand.
I used to sleep a whole night through, awake
to what came next that I rushed to. Those nights
are gone, it seems, and it's my current fate
to wake inside the next day's empty blight
of hours before the dawn to hear the hum
and pulse inside my head, inside the walls,
to see the solitude of shoes, the dumb
materiality of rooms, the pall
before the light begins again. Ghosts tell
me tales within the silence of this spell.

Up Too Early

The train, a bird at 5 a.m., and then
the vast hole of the night, and then again
that single song I wanted to count on,
a two-note call, but then the song is gone.
So what I have is first light of the day,
the backsides of three cars across the way,
the high-pitched background whine inside my head,
the life ahead and all the past that's dead
that lives like busy ghosts awaiting me
to join them in another's memory.
Sometimes I think a pair of ragged claws
is not an awful fate. At least the laws
of such a state do not require a mind,
just instinct's twitch that lives outside of Time.

What Waits

Predawn. Two armadillos scurry 'cross
the lit up nighttime lawn with armored hides,
short tails like little whips. Few steps they're lost
amid some underbrush. The world outside.
The birds on poles await the silent wires
that mean we're gone. The gators bide their time
with slow reptilian hearts that do not tire.
For what a mess we've made, we with our minds
who've cracked so many codes except our own
demented souls', our tribal fears, our lust
to get our pound of flesh, our brittle bones
that reason not the need, our deep mistrust
of love. And so the birds and gators wait,
as patient as the tigers at the gate.

Like This
(for MR)

Dawn's rouge, a hint, is gone. The first or last
of fire in the sky? There's gray above
the trees, then sharpened winter blue. I'd ask
what all this is, but I'll know soon enough.
Up in Vermont, a poet sits in front
of fire. Her back can feel the seeping cold.
So much of it's like this, she thinks, the blunt
force and the constant theft. It makes you old.
Outside, the mountains, colder than the moon,
the black trees with their weight of snow, the air
that tears the lungs. This clarity's the boon
she seeks, beyond what's wrong, what's right, what's fair.
Doth feelingly persuade me who I am. . . .
Words rise like sparks. Once more, she understands.

Coffee

The coffee's better since I'm using less.
I thought, the more the better it will be,
the stronger, tastier...and all the rest.
Turns out that's wrong. *Enough's* the hard-earned key.
Embarrassed into knowing once again.
I know that this must be the way for me
today, tomorrow, till the very end.
I have to stumble so that I can see.
I can't think of a time I haven't been
this way. I ran instead of walked. I screamed
instead of thought. Not once did I have skin
in any game. I didn't know I dreamed,
but then I woke, yet still I often fall.
Half-assed, I know, but closer to it all.

Mother

Up early to do laundry, Mother did
it in the basement when I was a kid.
How much she cared for us. How little she
could say a sweet, kind, idle word. I see
her now so differently. Time always tells
if it's the truth you need to hear. The spell
I fought my battles in the years have worn
away. She loved but she could not be warm.
Ferocity kept her alive. Control.
Control was the commandment in her soul,
for she had lost so much when she was young
that easy love remained a song unsung.
So hurt that she would not be hurt again,
her heart a wound that she had to defend.

Always Waiting

She's up before the clock erupts. The day
sneaks in at windows' edge, is huge behind
the blind's blank face where rain's last silver stays,
exploding in the first of light that finds
each drop that's left. A miracle of rare
device, he wrote, still seeing through his dream,
but I'm awake and there it is, and dares
me not to look at its exploding gleams—
though hard on eyes to look at beauty bare,
uncensored in the diamond light, the world
contained between the shadows' deep black hair,
a brilliance where the universe unfurls,
the door thrown open now to all that's there,
that's always waiting for us everywhere.

Call

The early-morning haunted call of train
is softened by the woods it lumbers through,
a lonely beast, a ship's horn in the rain
and fog, a melancholy, throaty blues
that's calling from another life, a voice
that's not a voice, like something in a dream
you've never seen that says you have no choice,
dark blaring from a ponderous machine.
Four hours on the train sounds out once more
as rain lace-curtains down and lightly drums
the roof and splatters on the stone. Some lore
about what Time is for, the journey from
and to, is in this rain-soaked basso call,
this summoning and farewell too, to all.

Difficult

The morning's difficult with wind and gray,
confusion in the trees, a dim and bare
bulb almost-light. The blue's been swept away,
the sky a cataract that blindly stares.
Ten minutes more, there's blue where gray has thinned,
small pools of it that now are almost gone.
I know this undecided place, chagrined,
between two choices, both of which are wrong,
or one's not wrong but just not right enough.
When did you understand that this is not
a perfect world, that most of it is bluff
(which, oddly, comes from *brag*) and less a plot
than tangled skein that some think they control?
You had to crack in order to be whole?

The Spark

The cardinal proclaims that life goes on,
although the gray-white sodden air is bleached
and strange. The bird's insistent call is calm
amid the post-rain gleam the sky has reached.
This morning feels like afternoon, the day,
somehow, collapsed into itself. The light
gave up, decided not to try—decay,
not opening, so day crawls toward the night.
So odd to wake to this... *completion*... gloom
that has a grainy silvered streak. The bird,
again, a trill that's woven on air's loom,
now sings his song with all his strength—the urge
that lusts for life, that holds us through the dark
calls out. Against this loss of light, this spark.

Exempt From Death

It rained last night. The branches feel the weight
of it, humpbacked, bowed down, and deep dark green.
The stream is still as sleep, and all awaits
what's on its way to shatter this sweet dream
of dawning light and rain-soaked world. The train's
horn haunts the heavy air, exempt from death
like memories of Saturday, whose name,
alone, could lift my heart, a cleansing breath
of life—of hours on my bike to see
new streets, discover what I'd missed last time,
or walk until my legs said *stop* past trees
and homes and stores—all mysteries, a kind
of... *holiness* that brought the world alive
for me, who hid in order to survive.

Up From Sleep

Just up from sleep and pillow-peace. Outside
more wind in trees, gray air right on the cusp
of blue. Not yet, but soon. Brand new, untried,
these hours of life. I yawn, the sweet sleep-dust
still in my eyes, my shoulders too still feel
the downward pulling weight of dream. Outside,
the tree talks to itself, the stream's black wheel
is rolling west, a pale blue sky presides.
White gold blinks on, blinks off. Green leaves ignite,
go dull and wait. That's what trees do. They live
the long, long game, are patient as the night,
give shelter from the rain, do not forgive,
do not accuse, are creatures of the earth
and sun, their lives a deep and patient birth.

A Step Away
(for O & H & S & M)

A star up in the west, gold glow amid
the azure dawn. It could be dead, for all
I know, or still alive. We all submit
to Time. Now pink and blue, the sky's a shore
black space laps up against. In this warm house,
the girls are up, the clicks of forks and knives,
sweet apples in the air, the crunch of toast,
and so far, all is well. Again, four lives
encounter what's in store for them out in
the busy world, in school and on the streets.
The cat runs out, is caught. What might have been
is not, not yet. They're dressed to go, and sleep's
as faraway as yesterday. Today
is just beyond the door, a step away.

Signs And Wonders

A burning bush in early morning gold:
these, too, are signs and wonders in the dawn—
the stream that's hurried on, that's never old
or tired, no matter if the wind is wild or calm;
the lawn, deep green as life that's still one step
ahead of death—a hawk against the sky
comes pat upon his cue—all things in debt
to balances that still persist, though
lies and greed and ignorance are hard at work
to kill the world. The trees that speak in tongues
the rumors in the air, the truths that lurk
in shadows that are overcome by sun;
the day that's nothing else but promises—
all hints, a glimpse of tangled providence.

Not A Single Instant

The tan gold of the dawn is filled with song,
yet only two birds sing—they pause as light
intensifies. The gold cannot last long;
it turns to silver-white as dawn turns ripe
and morning opens up. Last night a friend
was fretting on the phone—*There's this, there's that,
and then he said, and I don't want.* . . . No end
to how we waste our only life. The vast
blue sky's indifferent to mites
and dinosaurs, and gold is here and then
it's not. The wisest is a neophyte,
and not a single instant comes again.
Will I see how much life I waste today?
What won't I know when Time takes light away?

Spring / Summer

What's Coming

Beneath the roof of gray there's blue, and light
comes from the west. It's cold again, the spring
not surely here, the balances not right,
not yet, though spring birds have begun to sing.
The future's always almost here and then
it is and flows into the infinite,
the other name for *gone*. We wait for *when*
and hope and then forget and must submit
to *is*. It's cold this May. The lake is clear
of ice. I look across. The distance is
a new idea that never quite coheres.
The future trembles in the light, the risk
we yearn to take. Not now, but soon, the spring
arrives, and with the flowers all that Time will bring.

Arrivals

Took off in summer, landed in a spring
of daffodils and apple trees in bloom,
narcissi, and the cherries flowering,
forsythia on fire and more quite soon
of everything that wants to feel the sun—
the oaks about to burst out into leaf,
the maples too, for life here has begun
again at last. No more of winter's grief
in spring's new birth of hope in green and white
and yellow, purple branches simmering,
and, yes, two robins in the morning light
selecting twigs to nest. Were bells to ring
out from the blue silk sky I wouldn't be
surprised, the world exclaiming that it's free.

What Time Will Bring

The world is rising up, is bursting out,
is burgeoning, is harvesting itself
in green, in light that's not the winter's shout,
but kindness unconfused with something else.
And there's the heart that tries to understand,
that knows what it has done and tried to do,
and why it failed. Except for love, all plans
are wrong and why they have to fail; what's true
is true again. We wish to find the words.
We learn that words find us the way the spring
is kind beyond what we have earned. The birds
are building nests that hold what Time will bring.
We kneel and plant. We weed and water, try
our best to walk. We've learned we cannot fly.

Cherry Tree
(for JBH)

Good Lord it bursts upon the air like love,
like flowers in a dream of what the light
might be in worlds beyond the good-enough,
the decent average, the merely bright,
the latest thing. No precedent but memory, and that, at best, erased and smudged,
revised to tame or blame, occlude the gem
that mind can't hold by miring it in sludge.
Besides, the spring...what does it do but *spring*
at us? Bud here, bud there, we sleep, and wake
to tree exploded into blossoms' fling
that fills its sky with pink that consecrates,
perfumes the air. You blink, but it's still there,
so beautiful that you can only stare.

More Than Sixty Years Ago

And here it is to hand that summer day
we biked all day. He was in front for miles
to some Long Island town two hours away—
he knew someone. The day was summer-mild,
the sun, the up and down of pedals' lift
and push, and every revolution of
the wheels another boyhood's sacred gift
that let me see and feel the world. Enough
and more for that strange boy I was to be
out with the only friend I had who led
the way, unconscious that he'd set me free
by asking me to go with him. Ahead
was all I didn't know, but I was not alone
for once. That feeling was a brand new home.

July 1

July the first, the *1* a simple shape,
as bare as nail before a hammer drives it
into wood, pure as perfect ripened grape
alone upon a granite slab. Air fits
around, adjusts to it, a single in-
stance of the world. The sun's benign by ac-
cident. And all that is lives on what's been.
We batten on our elders' dreams and *fact*
means *what's been done* not what a liar claims.
She knits a second baby sweater—white
and soft for newborn skin. There are no names
for Baby A or B. Not yet. They're slight
but living shapes whose hearts beat on a screen,
as complicated, simple, as a dream.

Autumn

Near

Some leaves are in the wind. It's just the start
of autumn's sweeping clean the trees. Not yet
the frantic tangled upsurged flight that sparks
and shapes the air into a flashing net
of light. Not yet the rush of leaves that burst
up from the road when cars slash by, or scent—
not pine but crushed sweet powdered brown—not dirt,
but resined bark and honeyed oils blent.
Not cold enough but winter's on its way.
The failing green knows this is true—the hand
that ticks the seconds off has never stayed
except in dream, and though dream rules this land,
the trees, the sky, the dark and antlered deer
all sense the change and feel the ice is near.

All The Proof

At last the trees are burning—yellows, reds,
flared orange in the glare-bright silver light.
Late day, gone pale. There's dark and rain ahead,
so now the colors dim, light's lost its bite,
and winter's gray is soaked into the day.
I wake to sky that's drumming on the roof
and chimes that are a harbor's voice that say
no sun today. Outside is all the proof
that autumn ever needs to show that spring
is like a kiss that happened long ago,
a mythic tale that only dream can sing,
a secret song that only your ears know.
The rain is falling steadily, gray veil,
a scrim of air, of light that had to fail.

Winter Geese

A crazy barking in the sky. Blacks Vs
of geese, in long and ropy staggered lines
against the frozen blue-steel winter peace
cry out, *Which way? Come on!* Some Vs combine,
some Vs go on their own, some seem as lost
as most of us—*Go where?* All seek a sign
that I can't see or hear or sense across
the cold blue space, some natural design
beyond what I can know. Their calls are what
I recognize. I hear them deep inside
my mind and feel them knotted in my gut—
Which way is right? And how should I decide?
It's ink-black now. I go out once again
and hear more cries. My heart flies out to them.

The End Of Day

The clouds move east in autumn light, so rich
in darkened tones of gold and gray, the blue
beyond all name, the pink a witch's trick
to break your heart, like love that's not renewed.
And now, sun almost done, sky gone to gray,
green's on the cusp of black: the day has turned
its back as night seeps through the light's decay
and bulbs blink on, today's demise confirmed.
So black the wind through trees. The traffic cries
for home, a kiss, a drink, the privacy of love,
the questions there're no answers for, the rise
and fall of love's sweet breast, the sudden rush
that gets you through another day. You sleep.
The night brings stars as bright as sleep is deep.

Autumn Rain

The autumn rain that strips the trees arrived
last night. It's colder now than yesterday.
November's on its way, and I'm surprised
again. My birthday month's a week away.
A spreading circle of blown leaves beneath
the tree whose bones are showing more and more—
as dark and tough as what confronts belief,
the fact that says an ocean has a shore.
With rain, the wind is up, so what is weak
goes first. This is fall's winnowing. The sky
is dirty gray with threat. The winter, bleak
as ice on stone, is what is signified.
I sip my coffee, warm inside my home
and am so grateful that I'm not alone.

Day's End

Autumn By The River

Black mirror of the river sweeps across
and down the falls to crash in frothing white,
but cannot reassemble since it's tossed
and torn by rocks, and all its broken might's
constricted and convulsed by tree-lined banks
the river once carved out. I'm sitting in
its shattering, a roar beyond all thanks,
appeals, or any human word for sin,
for grace, for meanness or for charity,
for wisdom or for pleasure wrought by pain,
by fools mistaking Truth for clarity,
or profit trumping decency to gain
a penny more. This roar is something else,
a god's demand that's greater than a self.

Can't Sleep

Why is the tick of Time so loud at night,
so slow the hour hand, so deep the black
that seals the house, so deaf and blind the sight
that stares outside as nothing stares right back?
I know that Time moves on, but it's the...*depth*
of each long minute's span, the endlessness
that presses on the window panes, my breath
that seems the least important thing, unless
it is the chair. I read what Ishmael says—
baroque black humor tells the knotted tale
of Ahab's rage, the *Pequod*'s shattered death—
a small bright light illuminates the whale's
scarred, harpooned back that breeches on the page,
while I'm marooned in night's hermetic cage.

The Gloaming

It's five, late afternoon, the earth aslant
to sun, so light's a stripe across the tree
that's otherwise gone dark. The world is scant
of light, and what now shines is light's debris.
Quite still, the egrets glow in crystal gray,
their white a startling fact. A quiet time,
the shadows soft and pink far west, arrayed
across huge clouds, the day in its decline.
Now afterglow, the westering, the way
another day slips by, and what we said
or didn't say, our insights or dismay
are raveled in the gloaming of our bed.
A bird cries out as evening settles in—
another place another day begins.

But Not

The end of day. The sky is silver-gray.
The trees have lost the colors of their change,
their dying tapestries, the red arrays
and oranges that glow and are as strange
as dark that comes to finish day in night.
Two days ago a tree was filled with fire
the setting sun turned rust and orange bright
but smoldering, a seizure of desire.
I'd never seen the like of it, a tree
but not a tree, a radiance of smoke
that wasn't smoke—it was the light set free,
become as holy as the human hope
to feel the pulse of life. That was the last
of light, a blessing that arrived, unasked.

Death / Afterwards

Before The End

The cost of opening the grave. The cost
of death certificates, gratuities
for those who drive the limousines. The fees
to fly both there and back. And those who're lost
in grief, adrift because of Time's raw theft,
awed strangers to the body on the bed,
a much-loved man to family, now dead
as ice, his spirit flown. This is what's left.
Remains. Before the end he kissed goodbye
each one he loved—his dying need was love
he gave to those he'd leave behind. A tough
man with a simple heart, he fought, defied
Death's call until he kissed them all. Then died
after we'd gone. Let go, let Death decide.

First Night

She sleeps the first night by herself. The bed
is emptier than she has words to say.
How is it possible her house could be
so big, and vaster now than during day?
His clothes are still hung up, his shoes in rows,
his socks and undershirts still in his drawers,
his comb and tooth brush where they always go,
yet every single thing is changed. The doors,
the windows, rugs and chairs still in their place,
the silverware, the coffee pot are where
they always are. And everywhere a trace
of him, each inch a history that bears
the weight of his concern. She turns,
stays on her side. So much, ahead, to learn.

Billy
(After reading Mary Jo Salter's "Nora")

Some poets write a poem for one that is
now dead lost years before when they were young,
when bridges spanned much more than air's abyss,
and letters crammed to bottle-shape were flung
into the depths below. Such friends seem
consigned to death, put in the hands of fate—
call it whatever you want. They're a dream
that just we dream, words that we translate
from books that are long gone...as if the light
took shape as human, laughed at Time, then spoke,
transforming us by sharing its delight,
then vanished—bright fire turned to smoke.
The cost of such luck's brevity, thus loss—
its gift is undiminishable force.

Friends Walking

We walked for years before you went into
the dark. Two hours on almost every Saturday,
except for snow or rain, through seasons blue
with ease, through chances of the changing days.
We knew about as much as each next step,
yet chatted now and then, five-cent philos-
ophy, embarrassments when we misstepped,
and every word came straight out from our hearts.
We walked through autumn's stinging stained-glass air,
spring's upward thrust of beauty's perfumed face,
the summer's harvest days that steamed and flared,
and winter's cold—all, Time cannot erase.
We strolled inside the dream of youth. We talked
a bit, but side by side, true friends, we walked.

Air

This too will pass the old book says, and we
to shadows go along with all the rest.
The world renews itself. The current sea,
that bird, the very air—all travel west,
and, yes, the stones beneath the stream, the road
that seems so still, disintegrate as we
awake to life, or sleep in our life's code,
the secret way we tell ourselves to see
beyond the light. Amid this constant loss
we find ourselves through what and how we love.
Out of the dark, we journey to divorce
from life, returning to the dark. No drug
abates our fate, no passion or despair—
a bird flies by, is swallowed by the air.

More

What more than light that seems a song of ease,
a breeze that plays inside the trees like kids
who laugh themselves to sleep? There are the seas,
remote and difficult, whose winds forbid
the hope embedded in the DNA
of dreams, that redefine what *balance* means.
And there are evenings perfect as a day
that dawns in blood and fire and seems a dream
of how the furnace of creation glows.
Each dying autumn day, the wind-whipped ice
December flays, the spring's hot perfumed rose,
and summer's last-forever paradise.
Each time is more, and with each more there's less.
And then? About that we can only guess.

Winter

First Time In Days

The sun, first time in days, though it seems weeks.
Vast fragile dome of blue and light like love
that wants to heal by being what you seek.
As rare as that the radiance above
that glows against the window now, sets off
the mirror's silver sparks and streaks the walls
with alphabets whose meanings have been lost,
like words in dreams we heard but can't recall,
a something just beyond we know is there—
our shadows are a hint of it—a world
we glimpse and can't forget, a leaf in air
blown by October winds, a flag unfurled
against a dawning sky your eye just caught—
like what life means that came to you unsought.

The Coldest Morning

The coldest morning, brightest winter sun,
a laser light as pitiless as steel.
Perhaps this means true winter has begun.
Ice-blue and gray, the sky. Inside, I feel
the cold come seeping through the floor
and push against the glass relentlessly—
it longs to fill the world, this force of more
and more that knot by knot is now set free.
Somehow the trees look smaller in this cold.
Their naked grandeur seems ridiculous,
gaunt armatures of those become the old—
whose upraised arms are tortured in their thrust
towards light—see Kollwitz to see through my eyes,
and see the bent, the desperate, the despised.

Magic You Can Trust

A scattershot of snow is blowing in,
a stray confetti that's a warning sign
that more is on its way. It will take Time,
you think, for snowy winter to begin.
Not yet, but soon, a balance will occur,
and snow will tumble, billions-worth of flakes,
and no two are the same, like human fate,
both intricate and obvious—and more,
as brief as breath. An eye blink, and it's gone,
but on your tongue the sugar taste of dust,
the spice of sky, the strange attar of stone.
Just tangible, a magic you can trust.
Now later in the steel-eyed day the wind
is up, and ice, you sense, will soon begin.

The Heart Learns

I will not speak of miracles. What do
I know, except for what I see and sense?
Outlier from the crowd, I know what's true
upon my pulse, but for the rest, I guess.
I've been alone upon a plain that stretched
until the sky and saw a yellow glow
that's still bright in my eyes. And all the rest
I've stumbled through. Years later now I know—
at least I think I know—how much I missed
and what that cost the innocent. Time lost
is lost, but some things can be almost fixed.
The heart learns what's enough to ease the cost,
to stanch the blood, so healing can begin.
The winter trees creak in the freezing wind.

Weather For Hawks

White winter light and blue that long ago
forgot what mercy is. A morning for
a hawk. The clouds are silvered gray and glow
a razored glare, raw light you can't ignore
that blinds the eye that cannot help but look.
The perfect light for hawks. And when it dims,
the silver has a wicked gleam, a hook
that skewers nerves, edged pain up to the brim.
The wind is polishing the upper leaves.
Bright points wink on, wink off. We are what is
irrelevant. We are what we believe.
The hawk is real, the rest self-serving myth.
We wake, we work, we love, we war, we talk,
we plan, while high above, the circling hawk.

What He Found
(for JB)

How far the path in time and space, from there
to here! What sights of ice and stone and snow
and paw prints, moose tracks, and the green light's flare
you saw with wild eyes gaping at the flow
of arctic wind across a frozen land.
Out at the end was ecstasy that fed
the fire that raged that you could not command,
that lit the blood that pounded in your head
and cried for *more*. You only paused for love,
gold nugget in an ice-cold stream you clutched
with frozen hands that eased the ache, the rush
of your unruly heart. For you were touched
by nothing madness could explain and found
dry land when everything in you cried, *Drown*.

Weather For Hawks

White winter light and blue that long ago
forgot what mercy is. A morning for
a hawk. The clouds are silvered gray and glow
a razored glare, raw light you can't ignore
that blinds the eye that cannot help but look.
The perfect light for hawks. And when it dims,
the silver has a wicked gleam, a hook
that skewers nerves, edged pain up to the brim.
The wind is polishing the upper leaves.
Bright points wink on, wink off. We are what is
irrelevant. We are what we believe.
The hawk is real, the rest self-serving myth.
We wake, we work, we love, we war, we talk,
we plan, while high above, the circling hawk.

What He Found
(for JB)

How far the path in time and space, from there
to here! What sights of ice and stone and snow
and paw prints, moose tracks, and the green light's flare
you saw with wild eyes gaping at the flow
of arctic wind across a frozen land.
Out at the end was ecstasy that fed
the fire that raged that you could not command,
that lit the blood that pounded in your head
and cried for *more*. You only paused for love,
gold nugget in an ice-cold stream you clutched
with frozen hands that eased the ache, the rush
of your unruly heart. For you were touched
by nothing madness could explain and found
dry land when everything in you cried, *Drown*.

A Kind Of Dust

It snowed last night. A sprinkling of a kind
of dust, if dust were white and it could freeze.
There're patches here and there, all knuckled, blind,
and now more's lightly showering down. The trees
across the way, as naked as a bone
becomes, are slowly turning white. Old men,
old women, stripped, exposed, and as alone
as life that's been abandoned once again.
Dachau, I think, the meanness of the soul,
imagine what is coming down is ash
turned into tiny stars, exquisite, whole,
are answers to a question I've not asked
about the nightmare of our history—
why is it when we hate we feel most free?

Nature

On Hold

Sometimes, as now, the light's enough, the sun
behind a massive cloud that seeps like sea
across the blue. The birds are still; songs sung,
they're quiet, gone. The tree and stream agree
that silence is what's needed now—as if,
for this brief *once*, the clock has stopped. On hold,
the sky, the leaves, white flash of wings—this is
the world as poem upon a page, untold.
The fan still whirrs, and that is all I hear,
like water far away. The books that burst
with languages are dumb, and each appears
exactly as it is. The world's been purged
of Time. Is this a warning or a gift?
I think it's both, like any granted wish.

The Seers

A bird calls out—for food? for help? to mate?
The universe seems unconcerned. The breeze
is loose inside the tree, for now its fate
is to be tossed, to wave its arms, unfree
and rooted as it is, its disarray
the opposite of will: A big dumb thing,
it gossips to itself in its own way.
Confused and self-absorbed, it flings and swings
its sun-drenched glinting leaves; it nods and sighs
and heaves; it lurches, settles down, then starts
again. Long dead the seers who read the rise
and fall of leaves, who understood the part
they play in giving fate a face and name,
who felt light's weight and heard the words of rain.

The Cost

The birds work all day long. No holidays,
no birds'-day-off, no time to read or write
a note to birds in other states, no way
to just relax, catch up on news, get tight
with dear old friends. Set free to roam the skies,
they do not roam but hunt familiar turf.
They aren't free but starving all their lives;
instinctual, they live to scan their earth
for food from dawn to dark. What grace, their glides,
their arabesques. But truth to say, it's all
to hunt, escape from predators, survive
to search again for food. We stare, enthralled—
imagination's angels on their course—
then pause at the exaction of the cost.

Alchemy

I'll call it Polar White or maybe Bone
is what it is. Names fly like leaves in fall,
and both are gone like *that*. A golden tone
ignites the pillar's white, a muezzin's call
that beauty doesn't always flee, a wing's
brief glance, but sometimes stays so we can see
the alchemy of stars that always sing
and shine in silence of what life can be.
That golden hue is turning white, but still
it flares along the edge as sun and earth
are partnered in their dance through dark that fills
the star-lit universe whose fiery birth
now glows as gently as a mother's hand
that soothes a hurt we cannot understand.

A Deer

A deer walks by like questions that refuse
to simplify themselves, then disappears
beyond the window's edge. What is the use
of this? What is the use of love or fear?
You'd think an answer would suffice, but when's
an answer been enough, when questions mul-
tiply like fireflies that rise again
to dazzle and to break our hearts? Time culls
for us the questions that we're measured by,
the roads we do not choose to take, the scraps
that take us to our knees and teach us why
and what we do not understand, the traps
the mirror never showed. A deer walks by,
and questions stir like glowing late night skies.

Weathers

The wind is up. There's dirt that tints the clouds.
The tree is like a mother who's distraught.
This is the language of the rain—the shrouds
of dirt, the surge of wind, confused applause
of trees. And yet. . .and yet, the blue's still there,
the dirty clouds are scattering, while light's
a strange glare flaring in the tree, and air
has no idea. There won't be rain. The flight
of cloud, ascendency of blue, suggest
not now, though later on, perhaps. But I
don't know the weather's mind. I'm just a guest
from yesterday who's learned he can't deny
that weather of the human mind is vexed,
self-satisfied, unhappy, and obsessed.

Full Flight

Again the river rushes by, indiff-
erent as air, as stone beneath the moss.
I'm nothing but another thing, a drift
of broken tree a winter storm has tossed
into the river's turbid flow. I look
down at the water's fall, straight line against
the river's width. It never loved, forsook
a heart or understood or guessed,
made promises or compromised or lied
or told the truth. It needs no audience
or confidante; it hasn't ever tried
or failed to do. It comes and then goes hence.
The river's not a strong brown god, but steel,
a silvered gleam, the full flight of the real.

Cannot Be Appeased

Look up, it's there again, the circling hawk,
black feathered wings against the troubled blue.
As unmistakable as death it stalks
the earth, an axiom that has been true
before *before* began. It's gone, of course.
You look away, it slipstreams down the sky
as if it never were. Yet all that force,
precise and desolate, still terrifies,
still circles in your inner eye, a taut
and ancient form that kindles memories
you cannot name but know, as fraught
as anything that cannot be appeased.
The sky's gray-blue and vast. Though nothing flies,
somewhere up there's a fierce, inhuman eye.

Old Bones

Ghosts

How old that railroad whistle is, as old
as bones that wish for home, as eyes that see
how Time, like sea, erodes the strength the bold—
all youth—have always had. There is no plea
against the rain or gray wind's ash or light
that fails, but images of long-gone roads,
horizons that refuse to end despite
what life must do, remain—those episodes
that made me who I am, surprised me with
the wonder of the sky and taught me not
to be afraid. Enough, back then, was wish
that managed to be true and so is locked
behind my eyes that see the mirror's truth—
that whistle summons ghosts that are my proof.

Circles

The circle turns. What else do circles do?
The circle's nothing but itself and means—
well there it is. What are the shades of blue?
There is a list, and lists don't seem like dreams,
but all we know does not add up to truth.
You don't need truth to make it through a day.
Alarm goes off. You wake. And there's the proof,
the fact of it. What else is there to say?
My father said, *You're sure learning nothing fast*
and laughed with acid irony. That was
the closest that he got. Now he's long past,
who cried before he died. First tears, then dust,
white ash the fire took in its own way
in Florida, one broiling, sun-flayed day.

Not A Blur

We're young so many years, and then we're not.
A snap of fingers—if your fingers work—
is all our urgent youth. Then, what could stop
you from the unknown road? You could not shirk
your heart's demands, unhappy as they were.
Your hope was always otherwhere, a place
where no one knew your name. They're not a blur,
those skies, the road, deep woods, the icy taste—
no, no, not taste at all—*sensation* in
the mouth of wet and ice, a mountain stream,
what water really is. All that has been
remains like light, or real love in a dream.
Pain nails you now, another road you're on
while on the couch. Now, all and nothing's gone.

.

Before I Blow The Candles Out

The light I see suggests a word: *benign*.
The tree's at peace, seems reaching for the sun,
and blue now stretches everywhere, as fine
as silk spun by the sky can be. The run
to night's begun, but first and best the day,
the open door to all there is—the bad
and mad (more rife these days in many ways)—
the all-the-rest, which, together, may add
up to hope. Who knows? We come from fish,
have reptile bones, bad backs of hominids—
too often live like Calibans who wish
our sisters ill. The door swings wide and bids
me welcome once again. May all be well.
May all enchained be now released from Hell.

Domestic Life

The Fan

The fan is whirling like the background hum
beneath all noise, the heart's *lub-dub* beneath
the skin, inside its quiet cage of bones,
the busy circuitry that is its home.
As still as stone, the world is never dumb.
Get close enough and you can hear it breathe.
The fan's slow-motion, like the universe,
spins into what is coming next, like verse
inventing what it thinks it means from crumbs
it finds along the way, from light, from leaves,
from everything that's evidence, the all
that's left behind for us, the sea, the call
of bird that fades into the sky, the fan
a quiet friend who says he understands.

Hush

White-blue and still this Saturday. I see
the wind inside the trees. Infrequent rush
of tires down the street. No dreams for me
again. So long, it seems, there's just a hush,
and then I wake, and there's the sky. For years
I tumbled down the nightmare pit, my fears
made real in broken light, in choked-back tears,
in incoherence my mind engineered
each night. A terrible intensity
of doubt, a hunger's ache for something I
could never name, some answer that would free
me from that plunge I never could defy.
I know they're there, behind some door inside.
My oldest ghosts are still, but they abide.

A Shape Of Ice

(from Thomas Hardy's "The Convergence of the Twain")

What's happened now that drives the siren mad
to shriek through air then disappear into
the day's next reckoning? With all the sad
events and accidents that we've been through—
the list gets longer every day—the way
the hand neglects the blade that's sharp side up;
forgetful eagerness that shatters day
to glass and steel and beats the brain to pulp;
the step that's lower than you thought; the bag
that doesn't hold; the ease with which the mind
goes walkabout so whirling saw just snags
two fingers fast asleep and redesigns
your hand. We try. We hope we aren't blind,
though bound on a collision course with Time.

At The Dentist

Her son was dead at seventeen, she said.
An aneurism, middle of the brain.
She looked away. She never said, *He's dead.*
Her word was *lost.* What wouldn't be inane
to say? *He had these headaches that got worse.*
His neck began to hurt. No doctor knew—
they guessed. But then one day his eye was crossed.
One doctor said infection. Not a clue.
I exploded. He needs an MRI
and now! And I said more. He made the call.
And there it was. They tried, and then they tried
again. They couldn't operate. So all
that we could do was be with him for months
until he died. She had a *good boy,* once.

Montecito, California— A Photo From Above

> *(Adapted from Wikipeida: A series of mudflows occurred in Southern California in early January 2018, particularly affecting areas northwest Los Angeles and Santa Barbara County. The incident was responsible for 23 deaths, although the bodies of two victims were not found. Approximately 163 people were hospitalized with various injuries, including four in critical condition. The disaster occurred one month after a series of wildfires. The conflagrations devastated steep slopes, which caused loss of vegetation and destabilization of the soil and greatly facilitated subsequent mudflows. The mudflows caused at least $177 million [2018 USD] in property damage, and cost at least $7 million in emergency responses and another $43 million [2018 USD] to clean up.)*

The mud up in the hills. The surf, the beach
the other side. The houses, streets, between
brown washed-out heights and ocean's wild reach,
the hubris of the scheme, the scar a stream
that grew in force and depth as rain poured down
and washed the hill away. Had no one seen
the dangers of the heights above the town?
Had no one thought, *This is a dream.*
We're hypnotized. Am I the only one
who sees the danger lurking there that rain,
enough of it, will loosen mud in tons,

then gravity will do the rest? Insane.
That's what we are. Then turned away to mow his lawn and thought, *At least it never snows.*

Under Anesthesia

I was and then I wasn't here. I woke
with no idea I'd gone and then returned,
a brace around my arm. Designer dope
the doctors use. If you're still here, you learn—
the Caterpillar's wisdom is a pin
in our balloon. Two hours plus in a
parenthesis, then back where I had been,
a permanent lacuna in my day,
a meatsack with ID around its wrist,
two legs, two arms, and all the rest,
but gone the poetry, the light that slips
inside the words, a hair's breadth second best,
and gone the prism of the present tense
where all of Time shines forth as we fly hence.

My Sin

I'm there. I've closed that door. I'm on the road.
I'm running from my life, and from my sons—
yes, that's what I did. What did I know?
What did I *know?* My life had not begun.
The memory of freedom never ends.
The road ahead, the sky, the purity,
off on my own, the road my one true friend.
I was as dense as stone, unnervingly.
But no escape is possible except
by death, and death was not my goal. What did
I want? I wanted *faraway*, was swept
by unlived needs. My life? I was a kid.
I had no choice but choices that I made—
my sin is that I made those others pay.

Part Of Me

The more I look, the more I see there is
to see out there, in me, in me in it,
in it in me—I look and I relive
the road, the pounding sea, the far-off gift
of sky I didn't have the words to say.
The rush, the awful thing I did to her—
the world, my certainty I couldn't stay,
then out, then on the street, and in the blur
of being me, all I saw was my next step
as everything flew far away and strange—
the sidewalk was a dream, my life ahead
faint as a guess, as all the life I'd feigned.
A bird is screeching, shattering the air—
I'm here, though part of me is always there.

The 24th

I can't ignore the 24 that stares
up from the calendar, black graceful shapes,
the day that I was born. Twelve times it's there,
and each time is a shock. My birthday date
looms up as hard and real as stones I leave along
the edge of Mother's plaque. The long years of
her endless work, her strength beyond what strong
might mean that left her hard to love.
And were she here right now, she'd be the same,
unalterable as life itself, her will
the weather of my days and nights. No flame
burned steadier. It burns within me still,
corrosive if I don't take care, as hot
as some frustrated Hell locked in my heart.

Hard Day

The weight is somehow lifted off. And in
the sky a face looks out then disappears.
The breeze is scribbling on the stream how near
and yet invisible it is. What's been
had clenched my heart, reduced me to my pain.
That gone, as balance reasserts itself,
I breathe again, no longer not myself,
but some poor panicked fool one-third insane.
There's what you did or didn't, couldn't, do.
There's ignorance, stupidity, and just
plain *What the fuck*, and then there're all the musts,
thank God, the jobs where you will not be screwed.
Perhaps. With luck. And then I took a breath.
Woke up. Remembered that it wasn't death.

What We Learned

We are the roads untaken, roads we took,
the words we didn't know to say because
we still were numb. And all that we forsook
is with us still—that is an iron law—
but only as another loss, an *if*
we'll never know the answer to, a chance
that came our way, an unexpected gift
we didn't understand, caught in the trance
we called our lives. And what is memory
for us? The gravestones that we drag through Time
like Marley's chains because we cannot flee
the mirror's stare that questions what it finds.
It always is too late, but we have learned
that water's wet, what fire does is burn.

Our Tribe

The day goes on regardless of the plight
of man. And that is right. We are the dust
that spoke, that saw the will of gods in flights
of birds, but never learned, not once, to trust
the one across the stream who held his spear
as we held ours but spoke another tongue.
We got what we deserved because our fear
matched theirs, and then we prayed and taught our young
to fear. We looked into the mirror of
their eyes and, satisfied, we died. The hate
would now go on; our kids were tough.
The mystery was gone. We knew their fate.
So let the day be gold or blue or green—
what's true is what we've done and what we've seen.

Failure

The sky is not alone in being gray.
A world away a woman tries to save
her kids, herself, from Syria. Away.
Away from home that's turned into a grave.
She fails. She doesn't make it out. So much
is lost these days, so many at a loss.
America, so privileged, has plunged
into the dark, so stupid gets applause
as if in ignorance the truth is found.
It's anger, here, that trumps all proof.
Simplicity, confusion's voice, now drowns
the air. *I'm angry. That's the only truth.*
What's true is countries rot inside and die,
about which most are ignorant or lie.

Venice

The chatter in the darkened square, the need
to know, to talk—Mediterranean
time. Heels across the midnight stones will seed
Venetian memories, bricks made a dream
of Time in water's sacrament. So old
the stones we walk upon, so old and new,
forever new, the water's flow that's told
the time no clock can count, the deep *adieu*
of everything as grain by grain the bricks
dissolve. Yet voices still ring out at night,
the shops display fine goods. The magic tricks
this city has are always a delight—
for here the hard, the soft, great opposites,
have merged and offer truths to deepen wits.

Behind The Curtain

It's gray stares back behind the blinds, the face
of weather coming on, spell broken by
a chirping bird that sings against the threat.
I stare back at the gray, am in song's debt,
and now the tune goes on—five notes seem all
of it as gray resumes its vigilance,
as dumb as stone, as old as Time, the *fons
et origo* that all is built upon.
Or is it not the face, but more the mask
of all there is, an endless masquerade
of balances? If so, the Wizard's not
a cheat behind his curtain where he's got
his crazy dials and wheels. It's Dorothy
who looks but doesn't see all that she sees.

Again
(for AP)

What now do all the numbers say, the so-
called *values* doctors judge our bodies by—
our bodies, not the life we used to know,
the easy years when each day seemed to fly?
What do the numbers say about my mate,
the coffee-sweetened morning air we've known
the many years we've been each other's fate,
discovering in love we shared the home
we didn't dare to dream about? What were
the odds, since so much was a storm of loss,
so what I knew was pain, what pain conferred,
that everything meant nothing but its cost?
I'm waiting in the waiting room again.
The ocean pounding sand will never end.

Steps

There's light. And everything that comes with it.
The shadows all that is must have, the tail
the dragon drags. An atom, too, the bit
that makes the universe—beyond the pale
of sight, yet everything that is—will cast
its counter-self, the thing it's not, yet is,
like memory, the flag tied to the mast
of every single thing. Each step's a risk
we take without a second thought. What else
to do once sleep is broken by the need
to see and feel the light again, the self
as urgent as a germinating seed?
A poet said there're promises to keep,
and there are puddles that are ocean-deep.

Addict

I can't explain the dark that closes in,
but that it comes at any time—in sun
or cloudy afternoon, at night—within
the self, and all you feel is *run*
and disappear. You take a drink, you down
a pill, another to make sure. You're safe
again, you're bullet proof; you're warmly drowned,
and underneath there's nothing, now, to face.
No hurt, no mirrored eyes accusing you,
no fear, no dark—those shadows on the wall
are innocent—a refuge that you knew
would gather you, would wrap you in its shawl,
would always, always keep the pain away,
and all it ever asks is that you stay.

Before The Brink

Late afternoon. The western sun is bright
but mellowed like a ripened wine, a depth
the morning cannot claim. A deep delight,
this older light, an end but not a threat.
It is a welcoming, long shadows on
soft yellow-green, already yesterday
as evening settles in. This is the calm
of what is gone, what cannot, ever, stay.
The lawn's now dark. Last light is in the trees.
The grass is cold and distant as the dead
we love, as strange as North Atlantic seas.
It's sobering to know what is ahead.
The light's retreated to the sky. It's pink,
blue-gray. So beautiful before the brink.

No More El Dorados?

I sit one day. I sit another day.
The world is noise outside: a road, desires,
horizons fading into dream. I stay
inside. I don't know if I'm tired, or fires
I've always counted on are moribund,
and if that's so, what now? It used to be
I'd step right through the door and find the sun
on other shores and see all I could see.
I yearned to be where deserts are, where seas
explode with distances that poetry
alone explains, where simply just to breathe
brought joy and just to walk meant I was free.
Am I idling? Or have I run aground?
Are there no more El Dorados to be found?

Untitled

> *"It will be the right train. . . because it is the right time."*
> —Louise Glück, "Utopia"

The road is there despite the time that's passed.
Like words that cannot be unheard, heard young,
before the fact of roads, before I asked,
before I knew to ask, why he had stung
my heart. I hear them now, long miles away.
I'm used to how Time loops ahead, the knots
that knit me to my life, all yesterdays
the weft around which my life's warp is caught.
I look into my hand and see the stream
that rock and sky once made and feel her lips
upon my mouth, the kindness of a dream
as real as earth against my back. I slip
through centuries and see a green branch shake
and know that none of this is a mistake.

Love

Happy Birthday
(for F)

This long road started with your voice—so soft
I didn't think it real. I couldn't know
my luck had changed. I'd paid the cost
for years and years and didn't trust *Hello*
in velvet tones, as if the world was worth
another try. I happened to be there—
by chance was all it was. So used to dearth,
I'd taken refuge in the empty air.
Alone was safe. And safe was good enough.
And then your call. It's many years since then.
Our love's been torn and healed, and we've grown tough
in service to the oath we took, back when
we hardly knew a thing but what the heart
declared. Your whispered voice—that was the start.

The Study

Surrounded by her photographs, all time
is held, a glowing branch that floats. The gold
and red of her wild curly hair, her fine,
unguarded, trusting smile. The truths they hold,
as unironic as the wind, some few
still understand. I had to learn to love,
so clenched that only what was real and true,
what I could not deny, could be enough
to wake my dormant heart. And she did that.
I learned to trust her velvet voice, her heart
as genuine as meadow's grace, the fact
of rain, her hands' and lips' deep, ancient art.
This room, this desk's become my refuge from
insanity. Amid the storms, this sun.

This Human Life

You look, you'll find it all. Results of loss,
of victories, of halfway to a place
you cannot name, of lines you stumbled cross
and wake up now to fate you have to face.
I've never been an easy man. It all
was just so strange to me, this human life,
the point of it, when I felt I could fall
right through. A beating pulse means one survives.
I came to love when I was lost and found
in it the joys and troubles of the heart.
The welcome of a smile that's true. The sound
of her voice in another room, the part
where things go wrong because no one's a saint
and trying often sounds like a complaint.

Our Sunday

The peace between the lines, between the notes,
the spots of light within the shadow's form,
the peace of pebbles in a box, of ghosts
who love us in our dreams—though torn
away, they're with us like the jewels the light
discovers in the rain. You do not say
your happiness, for after day is night,
but who knew I would taste its fruit, the way
the noise goes mute while all remains the same?
The crossword puzzle's old tricks wait, its puns,
its symmetries, its challenges to name
the hidden words. Our Sunday has begun.
A butterfly is drunk on buttercups—
it dips and swoops and can't believe its luck.

Flight 235 From Atlantic City

White roses in his youthful hand. Great dreams,
specific, tease his mind. Lust's seizure is sublime,
enchants the secular that always seems
as dumb as dust, the old routines of Time.
All have luggage packed with hopes and clothes—
pink rabbit purses, everyone a phone.
He's pacing now; her plane's arrived. She's close.
She's just beyond what he can see. Alone,
he waits, bouquet behind his back. My wife
is walking up the ramp. I know that smile;
long years are summarized in it. My life
has found its home. The kid? I hope the miles
ahead are kind. I hope he's not afraid.
I hope she's wonderful, and he gets laid.

Knitting
(for F)

They'll have the hours that she once spent, the skies
above our roof, the innocence of rain
that fell as she with sometimes aching hands
knit wool into a baby's hat, the plan,
the languages of knots, right next to her
to check. They'll see the pleasure that she left,
refusal to be less than right, to drop
a single stitch, commitment not to stop
until what's beautiful is done, brought out
of air, of mind, of boundless love that they
will have when she is memory and dream—
the sweaters, booties, out of which the gleam
of her great, loving heart will always shine,
if one has eyes to see, beyond her time.

www.ingramcontent.com/pod-product-compliance
Lightning Source LLC
Chambersburg PA
CBHW020937090426
42736CB00010B/1175